SIMPLE SCIENCE EXPERIMENTS

WITH

OPTICAL ILLUSIONS

By Eiji Orii and Masako Orii

Pictures by Kaoru Fujishima

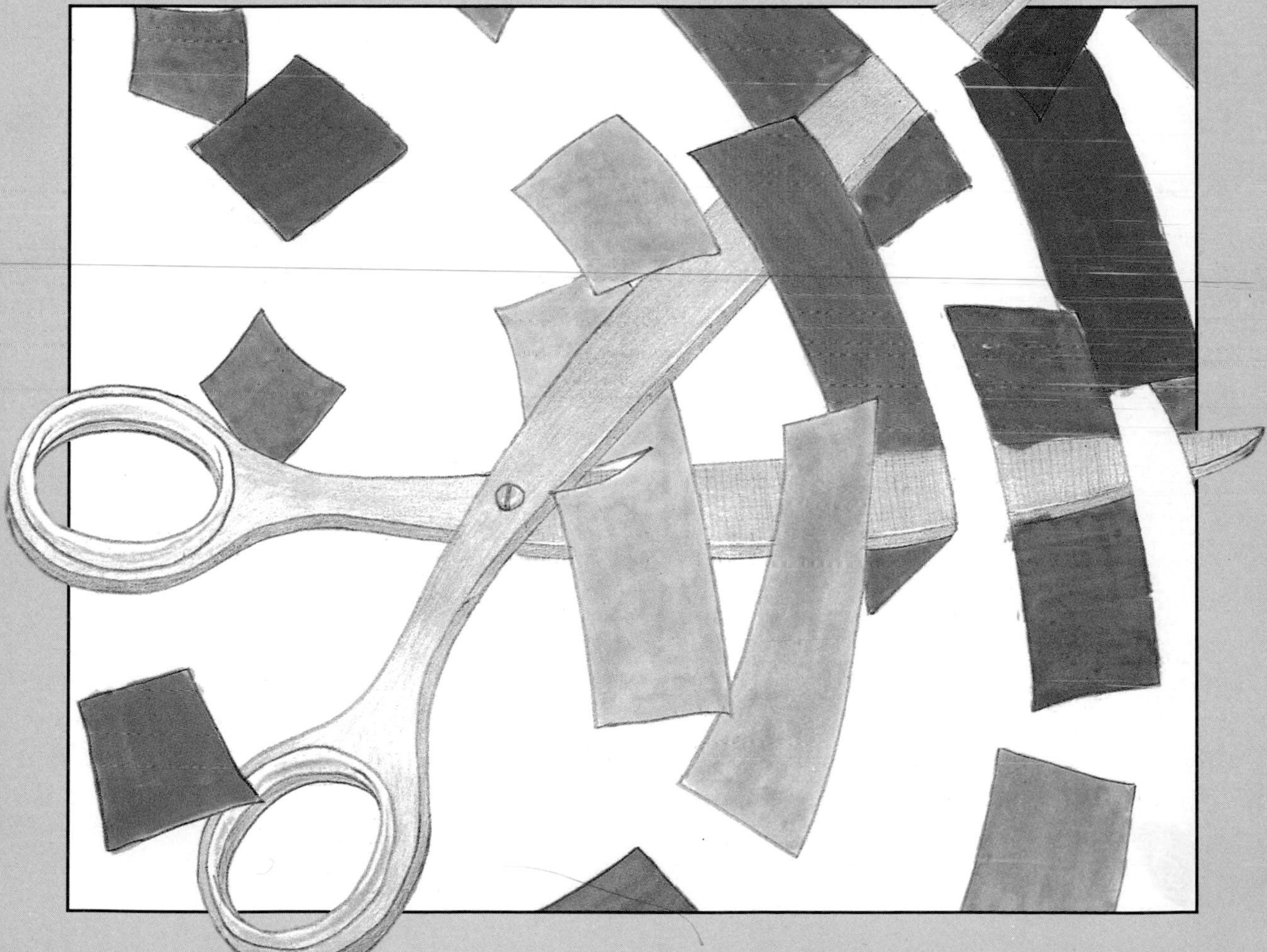

Gareth Stevens Children's Books
Milwaukee

For a free color catalog describing Gareth Stevens' list of high-quality childrens' books, call 1-800-341-3569.

Library of Congress Cataloging-in-Publication Data

Orii, Eiji, 1909-
    Simple science experiments with optical illusion / Eiji Orii and Masako Orii; illustrations by Kaoru Fujishima. — North American ed.
       p. cm. — (Simple science experiments)
    Includes index.
    Summary: Presents various optical illusions for the reader to
perform which illustrate how visual perception can be distorted.
    ISBN 1-55532-853-9
    1. Optical illusions—Juvenile literature. [1. Optical
illusions.] I. Orii, Masako. II. Fujishima, Kaoru, ill.
III. Title. IV. Series.
QP495.O75   1988
152.1'48—dc19
                            88-24756

North American edition first published in 1989 by

Gareth Stevens Children's Books
RiverCenter Building, Suite 201
1555 North RiverCenter Drive
Milwaukee, Wisconsin 53212, USA

Series editor and additional text: Rita Reitci
Research editor: Scott Enk
Additional illustrations: John Stroh
Design: Laurie Shock

Technical consultant: Jonathan Knopp, Chair, Science Department, Rufus King High School, Milwaukee

Printed in the United States of America

3 4 5 6 7 8 9 96 95 94 93 92 91 90

Every day, your brain tells you the meaning of something you see. You learn that certain patterns of lights and darks and lines mean that something is large or small, near or far, up or down.

But there are many patterns that you do not meet in nature. When you look at something entirely new, your brain tries to tell you it is like something that is already familiar. You can be fooled into thinking that you are seeing something that is not so. We call these confusing patterns optical illusions.

Lay a piece of thin paper over this page and trace the big star shown below. Inside of that star, trace and shade the smaller star. Put the book aside, and use a pencil to draw around the smaller star. That's not too difficult, is it?

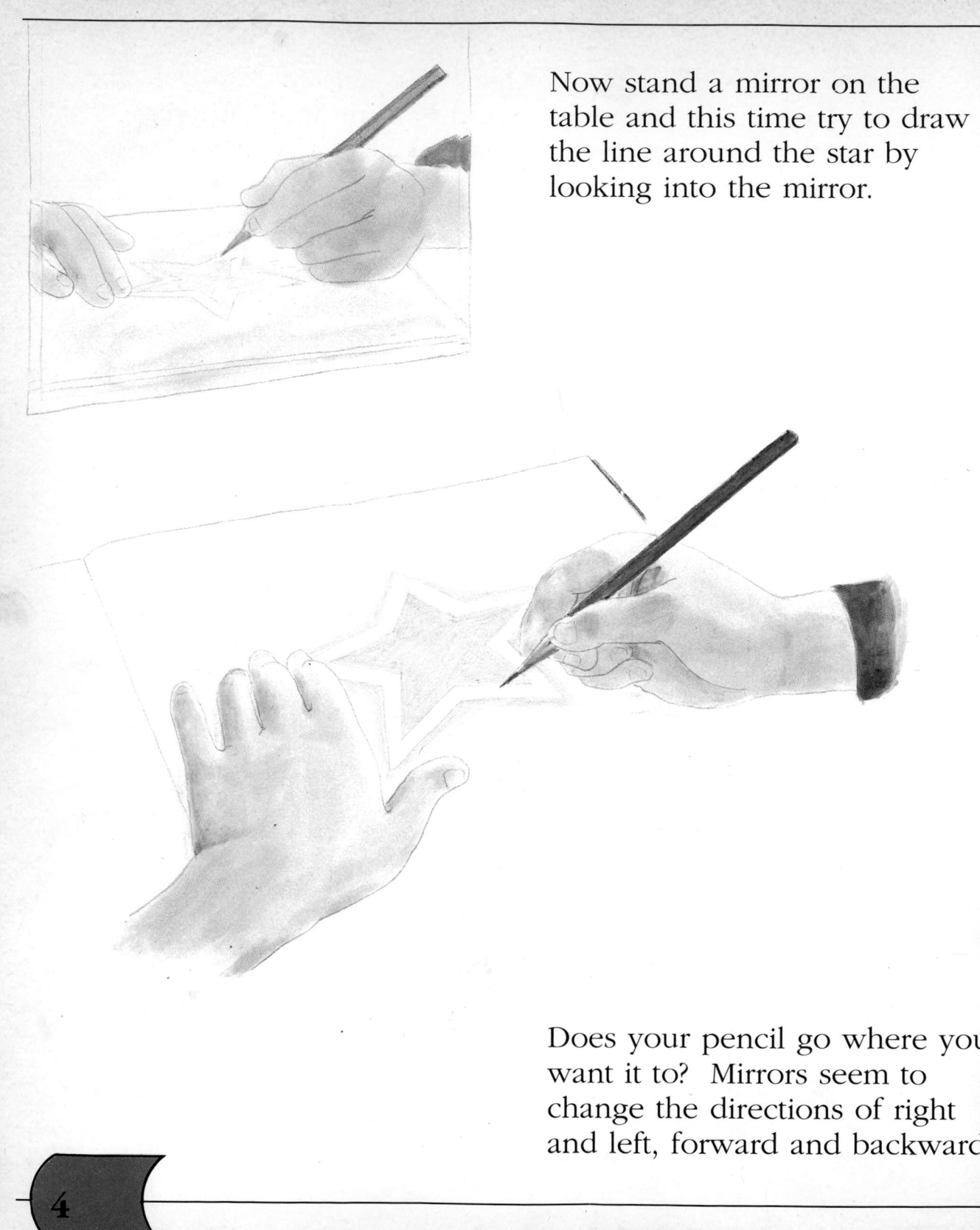

Now stand a mirror on the table and this time try to draw the line around the star by looking into the mirror.

Does your pencil go where you want it to? Mirrors seem to change the directions of right and left, forward and backward.

On another piece of paper, draw a twisted path like the one on this page, with a starting point and a stopping point. With a pencil, trace the path from start to stop. Isn't that easy?

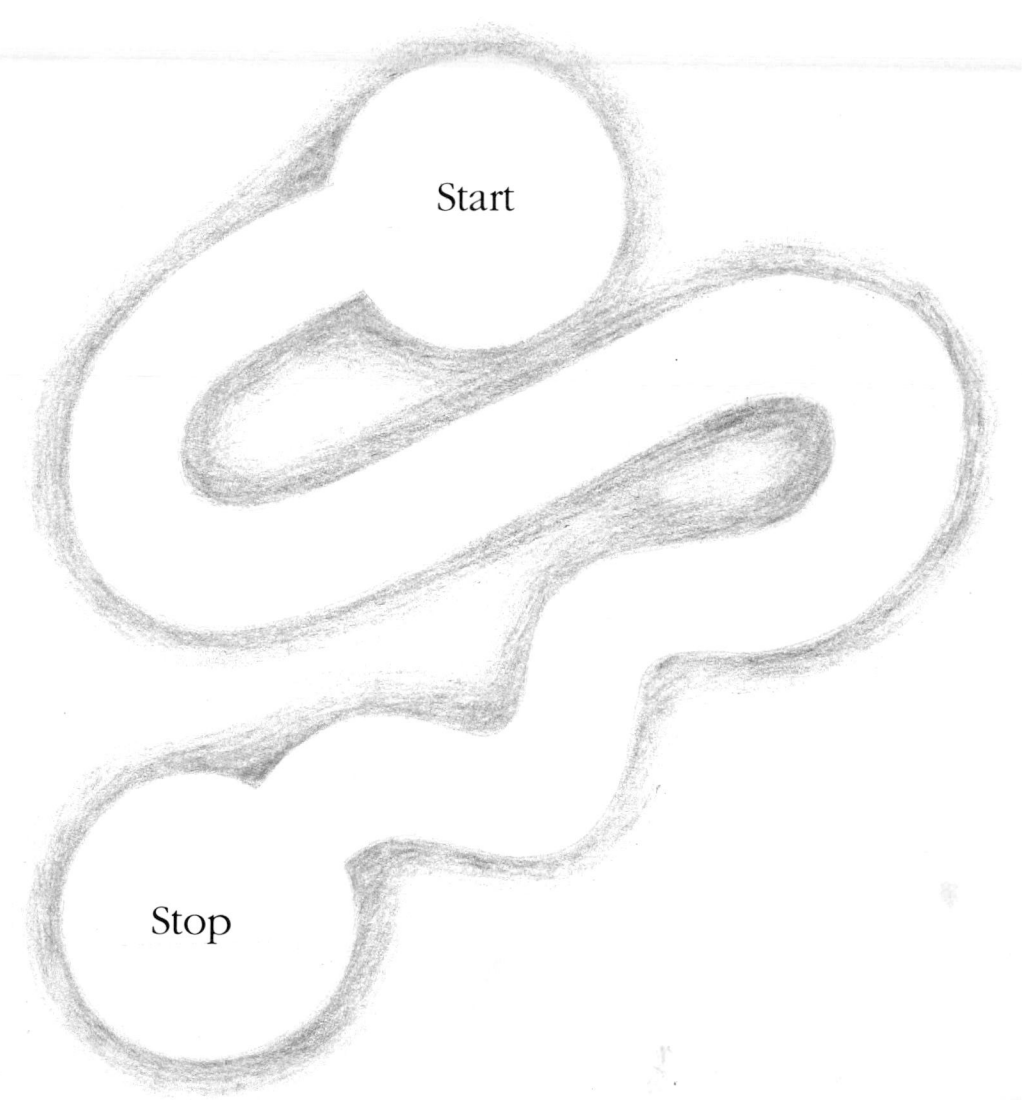

Start

Stop

Now put your drawing in front of a mirror. Place a stack of books in front of you so you cannot see your drawing. Try to trace the path just by looking in the mirror.

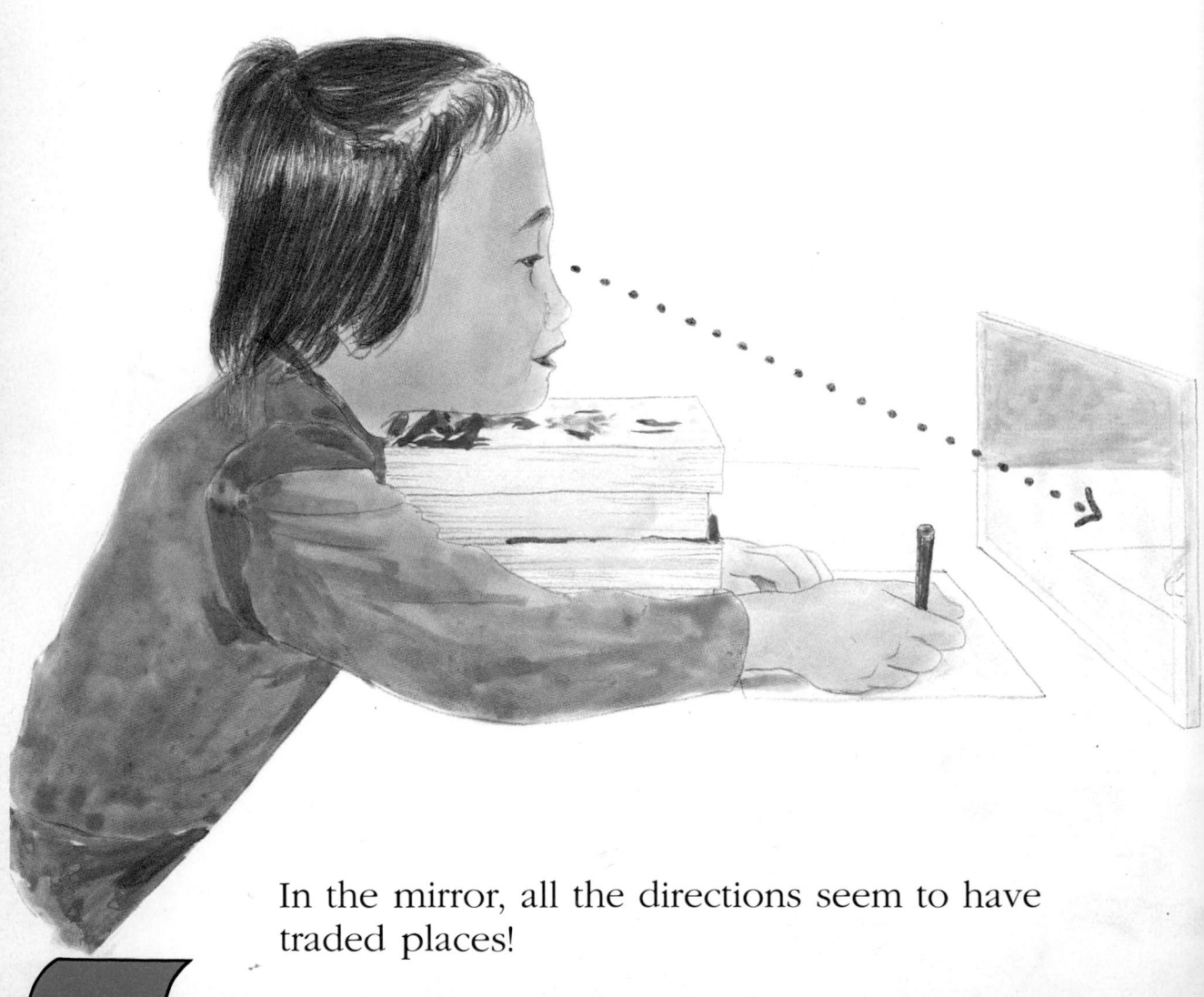

In the mirror, all the directions seem to have traded places!

Draw a big "69" on a piece of paper and put the paper on the wall. Now bend over and look at it through your legs. What do you see?

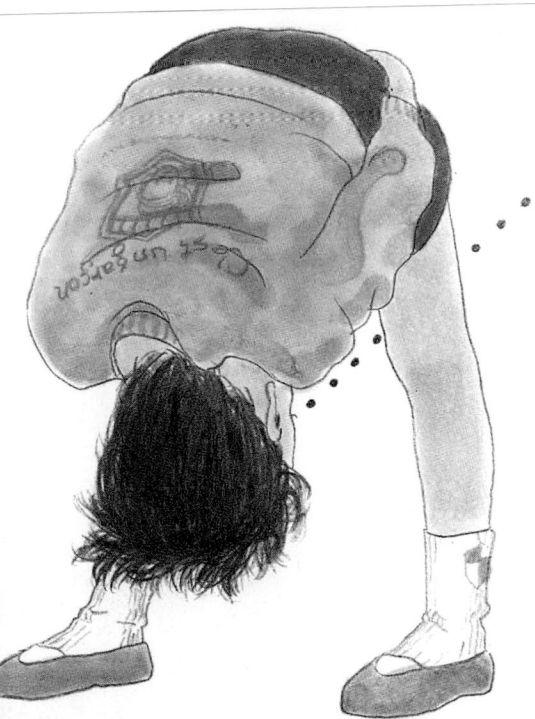

What happens if you turn the paper upside down and again bend over to look at it through your legs?

Someone seems to have gotten into the cake. Now turn the book upside down.

How did that piece of pie get there?

Here is a picture of a duck with little wings. What do you see when you turn the book sideways, with the duck's bill pointing to the ceiling?

Stand a postcard or a small piece of cardboard on the line between the butterfly and the flower. Then place your face down over the card. Look at the butterfly with your right eye as you look at the flower with your left.

What happens?

The butterfly seems to move closer to the flower.

Close your left eye. Hold up your index finger and line it up with a distant tree. Now open your left eye and close your right eye. What happens?

When you look out of your right eye, the tree appears to be lined up with your finger.

But when you look out of your left eye, the tree seems to have moved to the left.

Each eye sees a thing at an angle that's a little bit different from the other eye's view. This is how we see things as solid instead of flat.

Roll up a piece of paper into a tube and hold it to your left eye. Look through it at the things in front of you. Then place your right hand next to the paper tube, with the palm facing you. Now what happens when you look straight ahead?

Remember to look straight ahead with both eyes open.

Isn't that odd? It's as if you are looking through a hole in the palm of your hand!

What happens when:

> you close your right eye?
> you close your left eye?
> you move your palm up, down, forward, and backward?

What do you see?

Because each eye sees a slightly different view, we can play these optical illusion tricks.

Stretch your arms in front of you and put your fingertips together. What happens when you look at your fingertips as you bring them closer to your eyes?

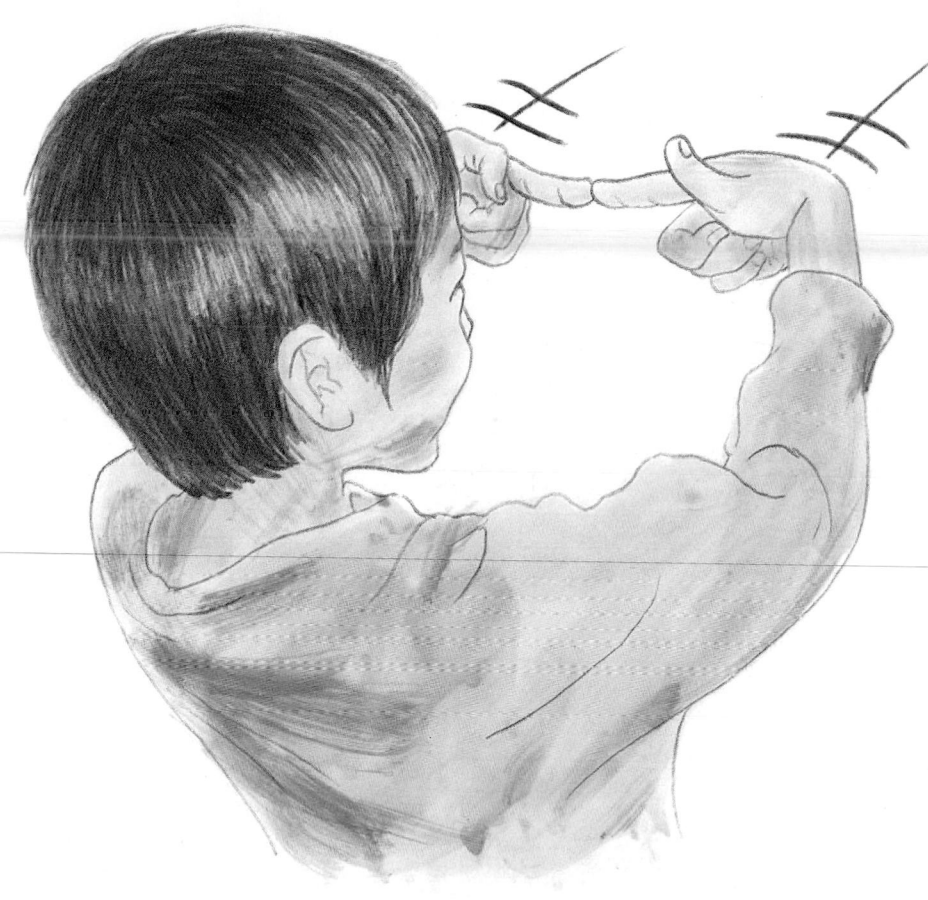

Your fingers look like sausages!

Fireworks make
beautiful designs
in the evening sky.
You can, too.

Get a flashlight. Turn it on and whirl it around in the dark for your friends. What will they see?

They will see a circle because our eyes hold the light image for a while.

Get a piece of cardboard and punch a hole through each end. Draw a goldfish on one side and a fishbowl on the other side. Loop rubber bands through the holes. Then twist both of the rubber bands tightly. Now pull on the ends of the rubber bands so that they untwist and the pictures whirl. What do you see?

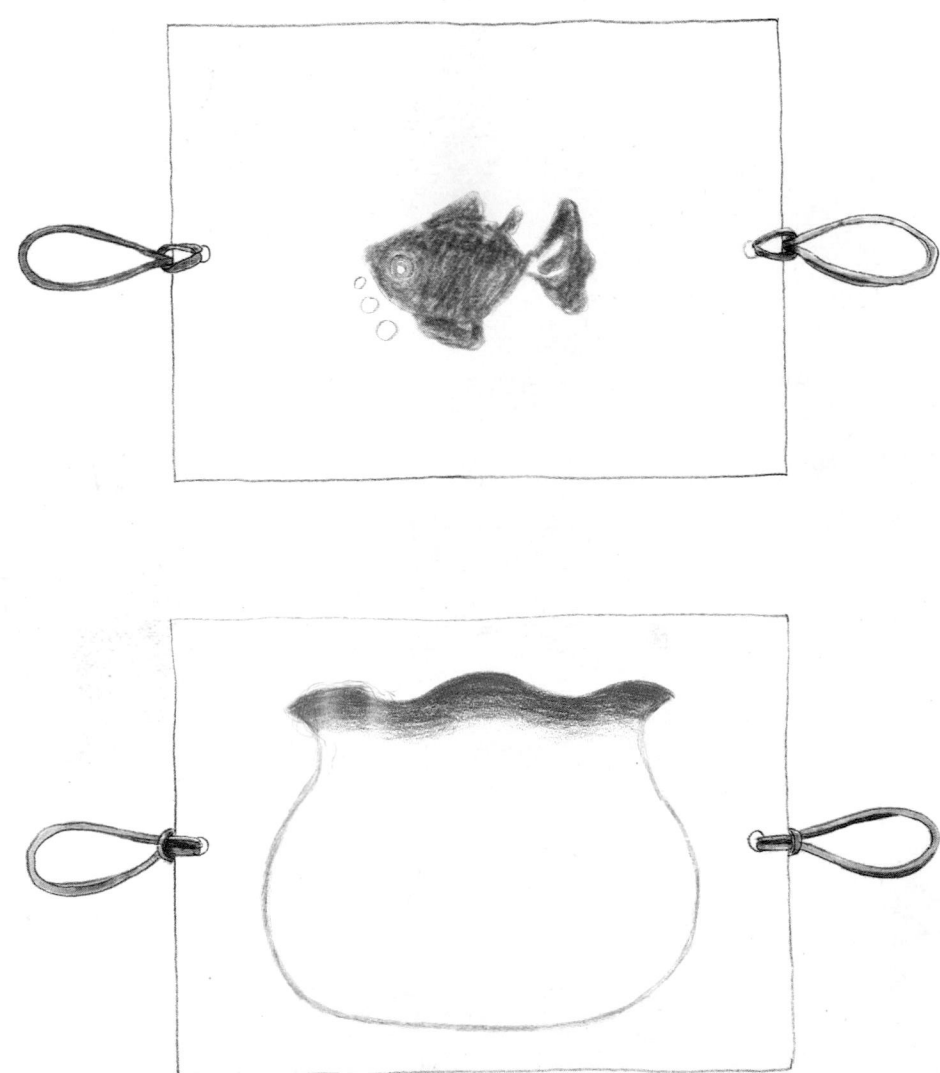

The goldfish is swimming in the bowl!

Our eyes hold a moving image a little bit longer than it takes for the image to move past.

Cut a piece of cardboard in the shape of a triangle. Put a pencil tip or toothpick through the center. Now spin it. What do you see?

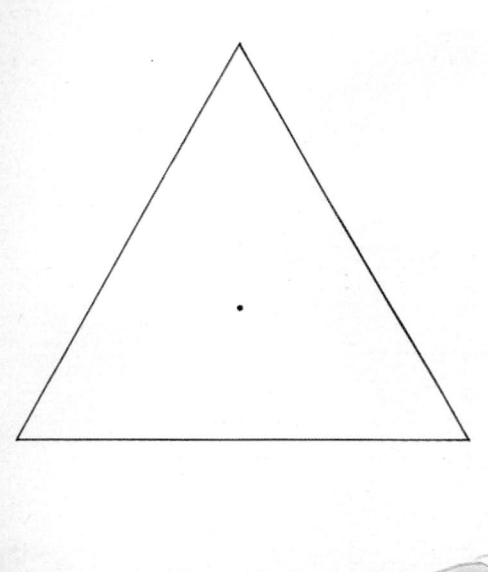

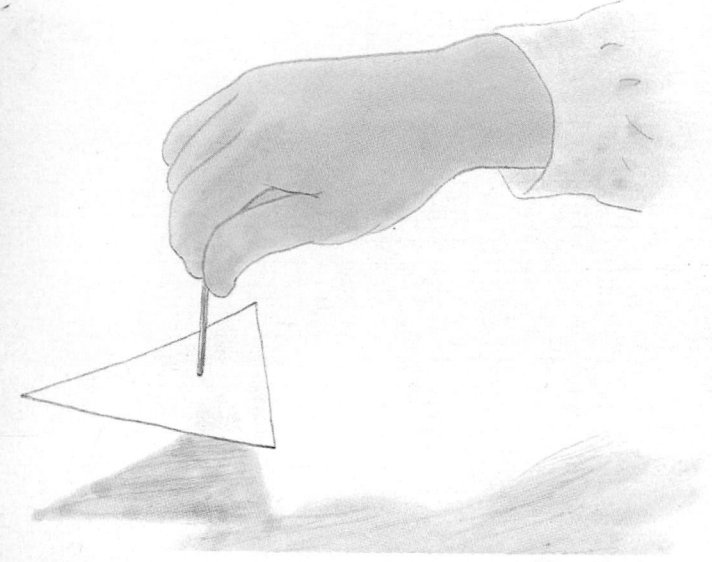

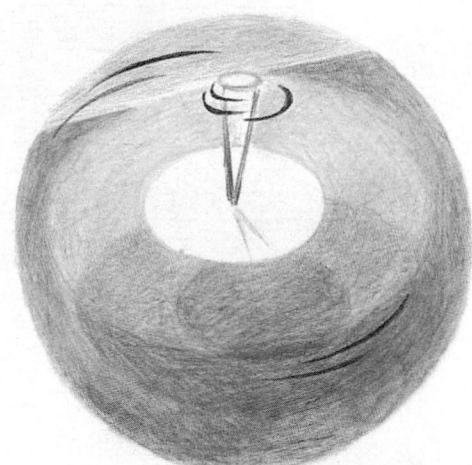

Now cut a piece of cardboard in the shape of a square. Put a toothpick or pencil tip through the center and spin it. What does the square look like as it spins?

We see a circle because our eyes hold the image of the corners as they spin around.

Draw four lines on your cardboard square and spin it again. What kind of design do you see?

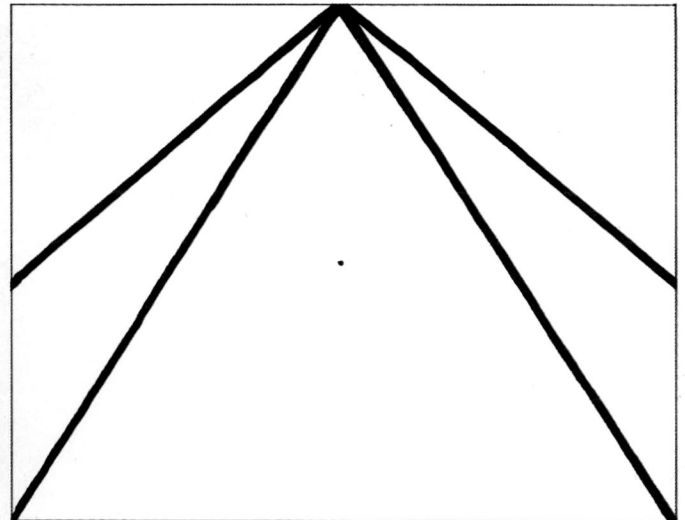

Draw two squares side by side that are exactly the same size. Now draw a bigger square around one and a slightly smaller square around the other. Do the first squares still seem to be the same size?

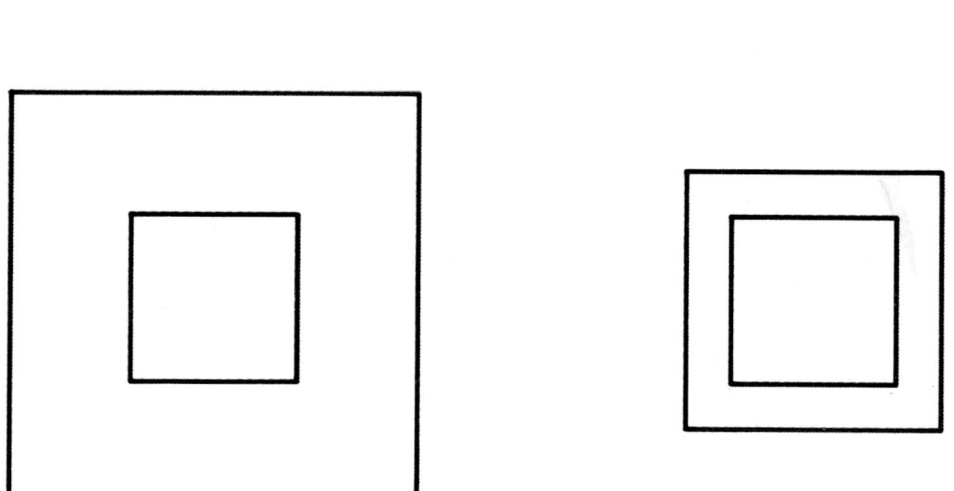

Our eyes are often fooled by the extra lines and shapes around the things we are looking at.

Using a large coin or a small glass or lid as a guide, trace two circles side by side. In one circle, draw some arrows pointing inside. Around the other circle, draw arrows pointing outside. Which circle now seems bigger?

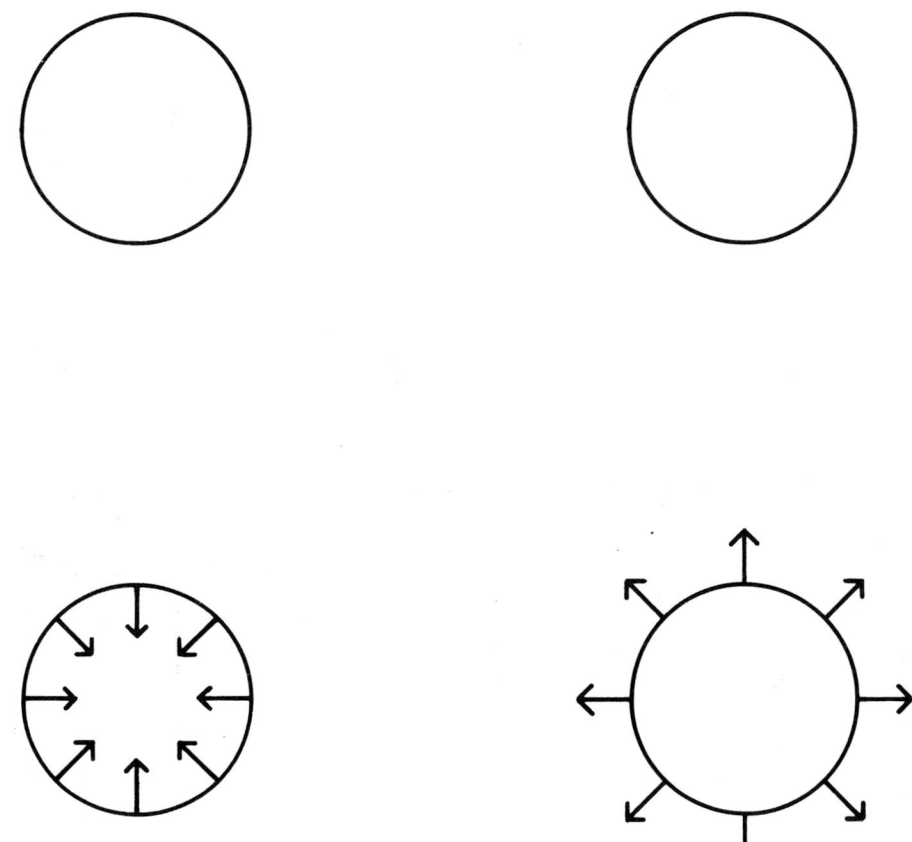

Different kinds of lines can make the same object look bigger or smaller.

Which circles on this page are the same size?

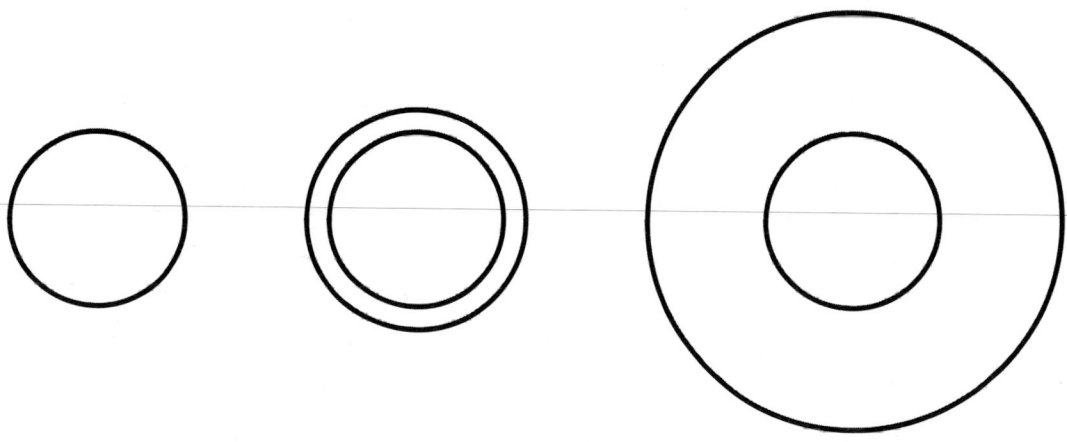

Now measure them with a ruler. Did you guess right?

Are the five slanted lines parallel to each other? Pick out which long lines slant exactly the same way.

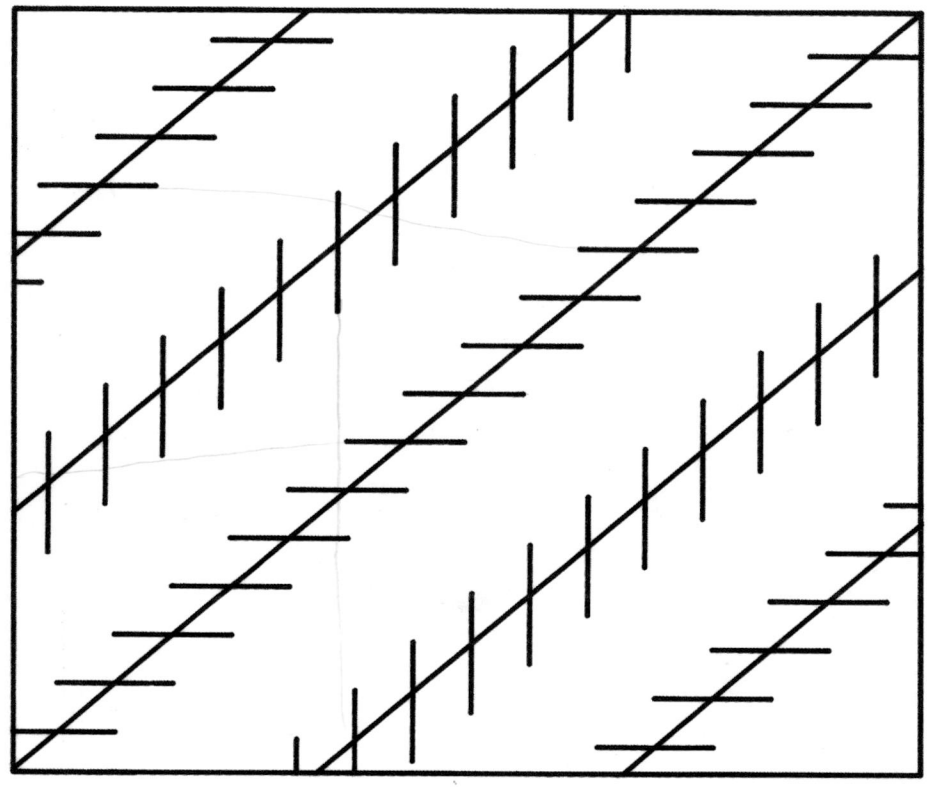

Now lay a ruler along one of the corner lines and carefully slide it to each of the other lines. Are you surprised?

Are the two red lines parallel to each other?

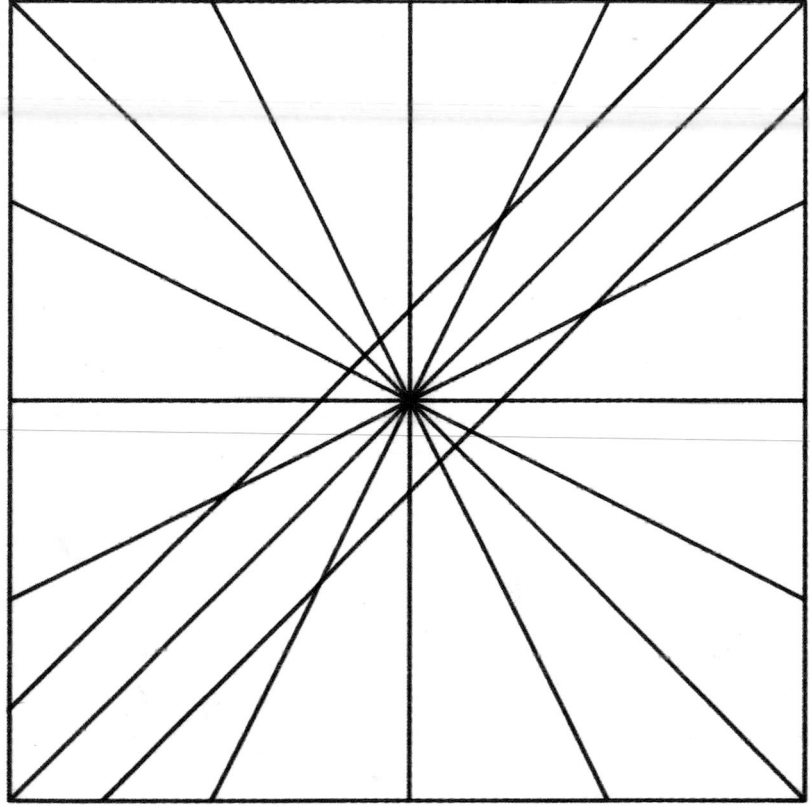

Lay two rulers, or two long pieces of paper, along the lines so that they go beyond the picture.

Is one of these girls taller than the other? Which one?
What do the lines tell your eyes?

Now measure each girl.

The figures drawn below are all the same size. In the bottom picture, the slanting lines of the background make us think that the two figures on the right are farther away. This tells our brain that they look smaller than when standing next to the figure on the left. So our brain decides that these big fellows would be even larger if they stood closer!

Because we really "see" with our brain, we have the fun and mix-ups of optical illusions.

GLOSSARY

Here is a list of words used in this book. After you read what each word means, you can see it used in a sentence.

design: a pattern, a picture
There are flowers in the design.

index: something that guides or points out
The index finger is sometimes called the pointer.

optical illusion: something you see that fools your brain into thinking it is something else
He thought he saw water on the road ahead, but it was just an optical illusion.

parallel: evenly, or equally, spaced and never touching; lines are said to be parallel to one another if there is an equal distance between them all along their length, so that they never touch; circles, too, can be parallel, as can a row of evenly spaced trees
When we park alongside the curb, we are said to be parallel parking.

sausage: chopped meat with lots of spices wrapped in a casing
Do you want sausage or soup for lunch?

stack: a neat pile
The stack of wood is for the stove.

stretch: reach, spread out, lengthen
You will need to stretch to put the books on the top shelf.

trace: to draw, sketch, or copy
Trace this design on the piece of cardboard.

triangle: an object or a shape with three sides
In music class, I play the triangle. It has three sides made of metal that ring when I hit them.

twisted: curved, with turns and circles
The twisted path wound through the forest.

INDEX